LEFT-HANDED KIDS

written and illustrated by
JAMES T. de KAY

M. EVANS & COMPANY, INC.
NEW YORK

De Kay, James T.
  Left-handed kids / written & illustrated by James T. de Kay.
    p. cm.
  ISBN 0-87131-591-2
  1. Cerebral dominance. 2. Left- and right-handedness. I. Title.
QP385.5.D45 1989   89-36893
152.3'35—dc20

Copyright © 1989 by James T. de Kay

M. Evans and Company, Inc.
216 East 49 Street
New York, New York 10017

Manufactured in the United States of America

"Krazy Kat" is reprinted by special permission of King
Features Syndicate, Inc.

9 8 7 6 5 4 3 2 1

Dedicated to
COLIN DAWKINS
who first told me
that most Krazy Kats
are left-handed, and
Ignatz Mouses aren't.

Left-handed kids tend
to be . . . well, a little different.

A little messier . . .

. . . a little dreamier . . .

. . . a little more emotional.

They're also likely to
be a little smarter
than right-handers.

Left-handers are twice
as likely to qualify for
membership in Mensa,
the high-IQ society.

Left-handers often do
well when they grow up.

Despite the fact that
only one person in
ten is left-handed,

Gerald Ford

George Bush

a full third of all
Presidents since 1945
have been left-handed.

Life has not always been
easy for left-handers. From
ancient times until well
into the twentieth century,
left-handedness was looked
upon as a loathsome and
unnatural aberration,
to be dealt with ruthlessly and
with dispatch.

with apologies to
H. M. Bateman

Any child who showed
a tendency to favor the
left hand was severely
chastised by right-
minded teachers . . .

. . . cautioned by right-minded parents . . .

. . . lectured by right-minded religionists . . .

. . . and vilified by
right-minded citizens
the world over, who
invented self-righteous
words to express their
approbation of (ugh!)
left-handedness.

Given all this social
pressure, most natural
left-handers were
forcibly switched to
right-handers.

Ronald Reagan, who was
born left-handed, was
switched. If he hadn't been
there would have
been still another left-
handed President.

Left-handers have a
reputation for being
a little ditzy. People used
to think they got that
way from coping with
a right-handed world
in which everything from
light bulbs to bottle openers
went the wrong way.

But now we know
that left-handers
are inherently
different from
right-handers.

It's not so much
which hand they use
that makes them
different. It's
which brain.

Scientists have long
known that the human
brain is divided into
two hemispheres, and
that one hemisphere
controls the right hand
and the other controls
the left hand.

But what they've only
recently come to understand
is that the two hemispheres
have entirely different skills,
different personalities, and
different ways of thinking.
Which hand you use
is an indication
of which side of the brain
you're tapped into.

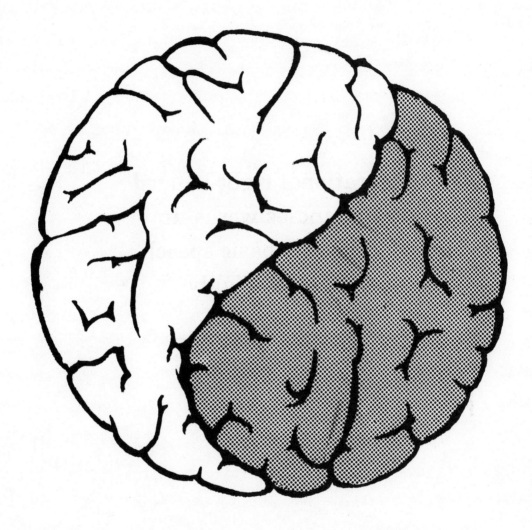

The rational right-handed
brain handles words. It
contains the basic speech
centers and is highly
verbal and adept at
analytical and
sequential thought.

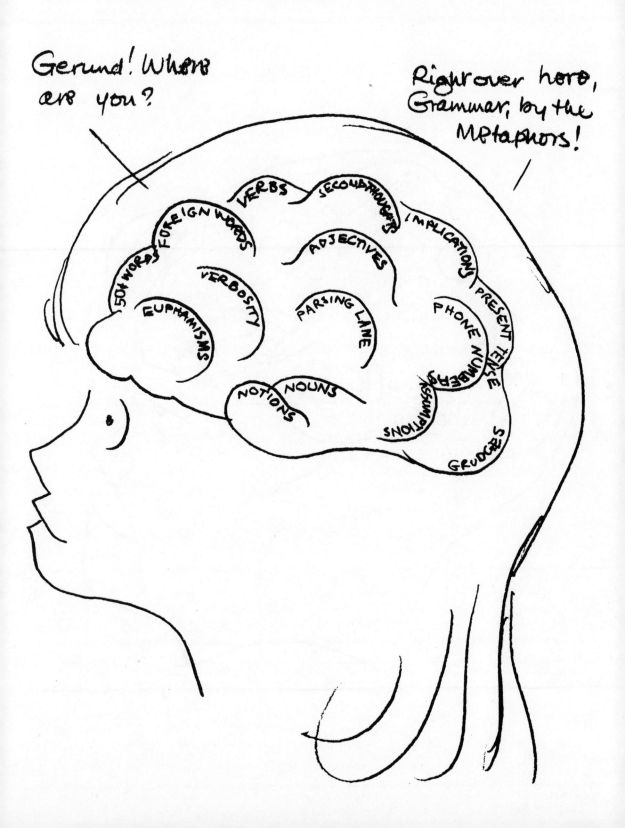

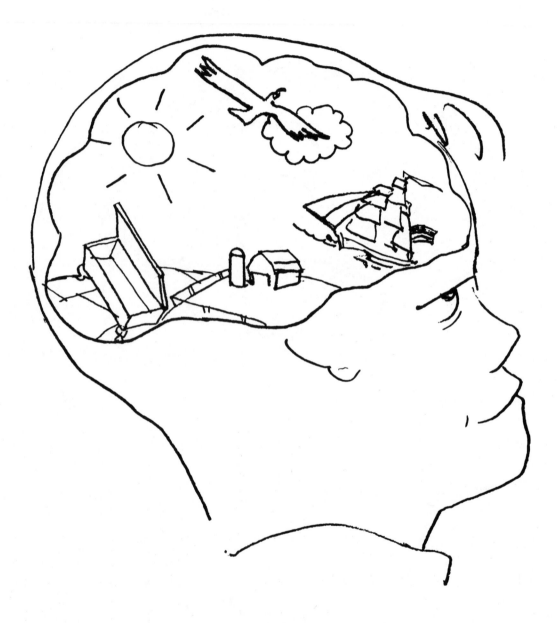

The emotional left-handed brain thinks in pictures. It understands three-dimensional space, music, tone of voice (but not words), and is highly imaginative.

The right-handed
brain is good at
school because
reading, 'riting, and
'rithmetic are all
logical, linear
disciplines.

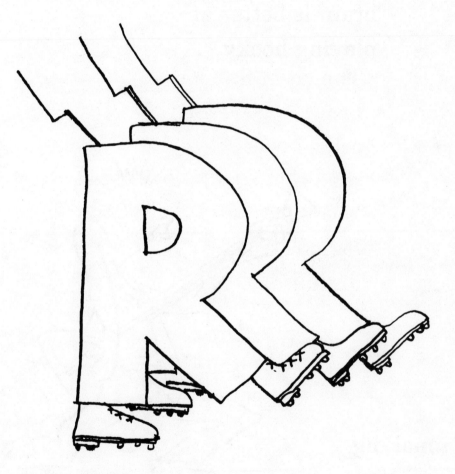

But the left-handed
brain is better at
playing hooky . . .

. . . making
music . . .

. . . drawing
pictures . . .

. . . and telling
jokes.

It's a fact.
Your sense of humor
is in your
left-handed brain.

It's no accident that
so many of the
great comics are
left-handed.

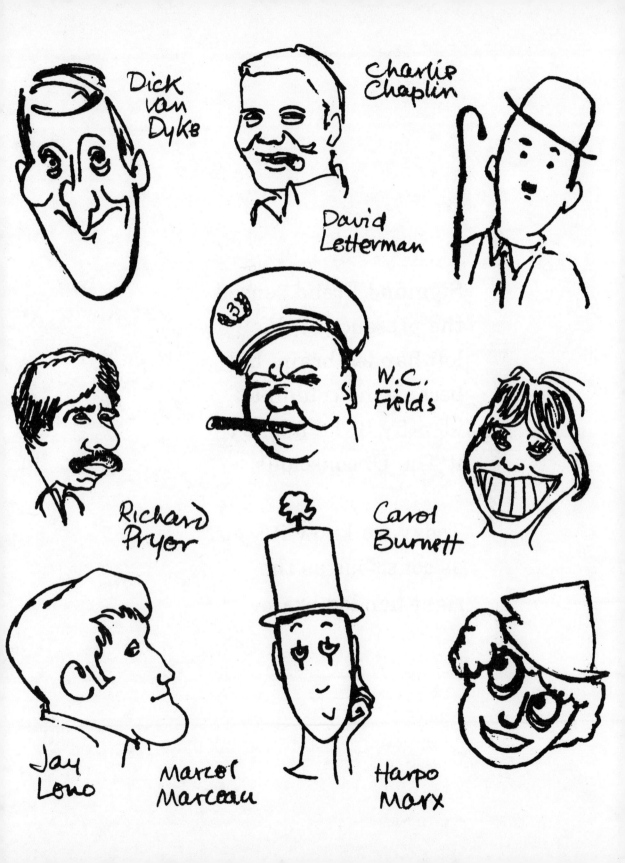

Dick van Dyke

Charlie Chaplin

David Letterman

W.C. Fields

Richard Pryor

Carol Burnett

Jay Leno

Marcel Marceau

Harpo Marx

Sigmund Freud sensed
the presence of the
left-handed brain, but
because he couldn't
identify it, he labeled
it The Unconscious.

Today we know it's just
as conscious as the
right-handed brain.

The left-handed brain does most
of our dreaming.

It's also where we get our
"hunches" and other "feelings" that
we can't explain with words.

The left-handed brain
is more susceptible to
alcohol than the
right-handed brain.

Which may explain why
left-handers are more
likely to have
drinking problems.

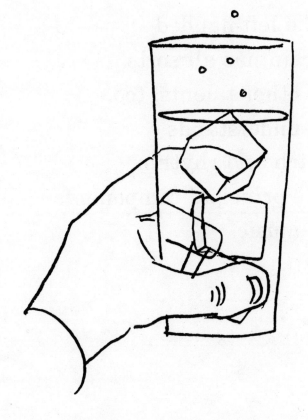

The left-handed
brain has all sorts
of other talents, too.
It understands
pitch and rhythm,
the principal components
of music.

Musical training is a more potent instrument than any other, because rhythm and harmony find their way into the secret places of the soul.

PLATO

Left-handers who
want a job in an
orchestra would do well
to take up the French horn,
which is valved
for the left hand.

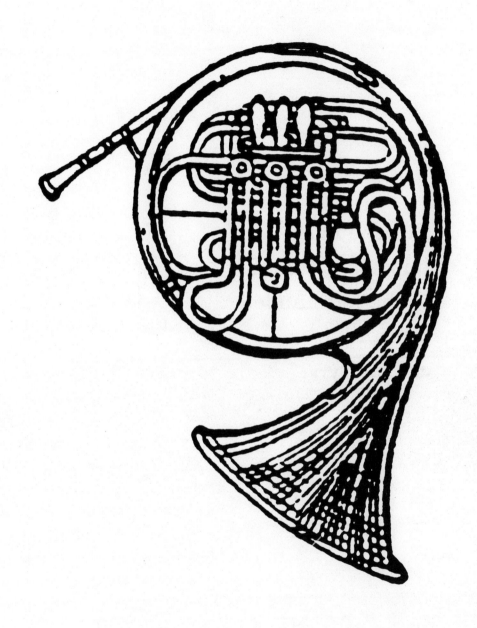

But the most
important talent
of the left-handed
brain is
creativity.

Contrary to popular
belief, creativity
has virtually nothing
to do with language
or any of the
intellectual skills
associated with
book-learning.

Words... do not seem to play any role in my... thought.
— Einstein

The basic tools of creative
thinking are mental pictures.
These are handled by the
left-handed brain; and
because it is unhampered
by logic, it is free to
make the kind of
creative connections that
cannot occur in
rational thought.

It is impossible to
think without a
mental picture.
        —Aristotle

Here's a famous test of
creativity. Your noncreative
right-handed brain sees only a
hodgepodge of disconnected
shapes, but your left-handed
brain can go beyond logic
and find the connecting
concept that makes sense
of the shapes.

(If you can't "see" beyond
the shapes, it's because your
right-handed brain is
trying to solve the problem
logically and won't let your
left-handed brain have a go.)

Here's another example, showing
how your left-handed brain
can even create things that
don't exist. It's called
Kanizsa's Triangle.

If you can see the white
triangle—the one with its apex
pointing up—it's because your
left-handed brain has *created*
that triangle to unify what
is otherwise simply a
collection of angles and
Pac Man shapes. There is,
in fact, no white
triangle there.

Michelangelo, who was left-handed, said "I have only to throw a pot of paint on the wall to find there fine landscapes." What he was describing, of course, was his left-handed brain's wonderful creative ability to bring order out of chaos.

After 4 years on that ladder, I think I prefer the pictures on the Sistine Chapel floor.

The left-handed brain's
mastery of the visual has an
important adjunct—it can "see"
three dimensionally. In Thurston's
Hand Test, you are asked to
identify which pictures are
of left hands and which are of
right hands. Your right-handed
brain is at a loss to handle
this problem, but your left-
handed brain can actually
rotate these drawings in
imaginary space to solve
the test.

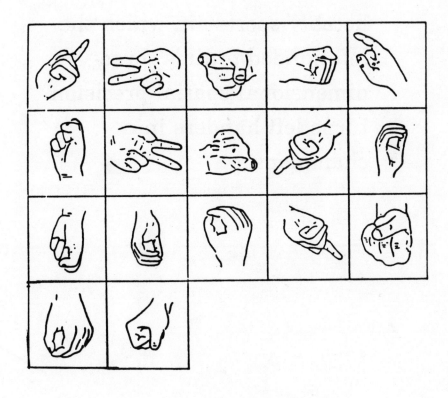

There are some activities—
notably sports—in which the
left-handed brain's three-
dimensional spatial precision
turns left-handers into
champions.

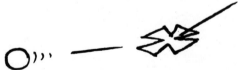

For instance, the
reason there are so many
left-handed tennis stars is
because Borg, Connors,
McEnroe, Navratilova, et al.,
have the ability to predict
precisely where the ball
is going to go.

For the same reason,
almost half the major
league batting stars,
and at least half the
pitching stars, are
left-handed.

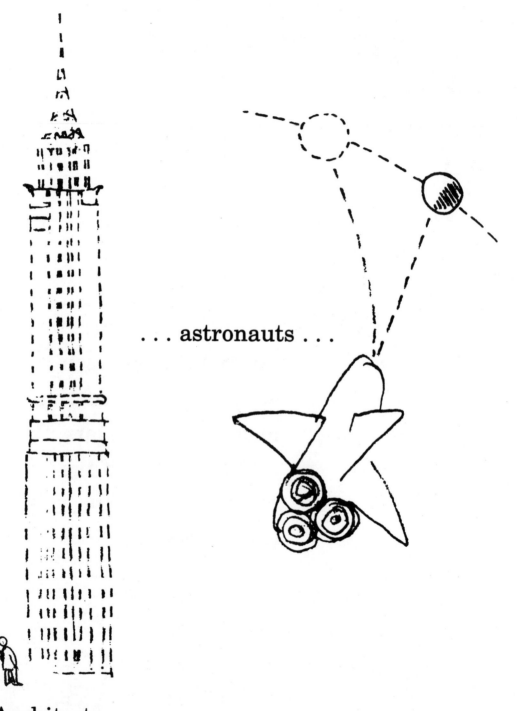

... astronauts ...

Architects ...

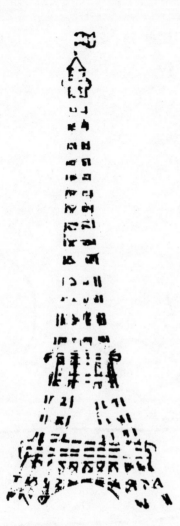

. . . and structural engineers
are just a few of the other
professionals who rely
primarily on the three-
dimensional left-handed brain.

Ever seen a picture in a
cloud? Or a face in
cracked plaster?

That was your left-handed
brain in the act of
creating.

Is left-handedness
inherited? Possibly.
We know, for instance,
that blond hair is
inherited, and there's a
distinct relationship
between blonds and
left-handedness, as
witness this quartet.

But while there is
some data to
suggest that
left-handedness runs in
families, scientists have
found no hard evidence
that the trait is
carried genetically.

Find anything yet, Gene?

Just some amino acids and a latent tendency or two.

One of the more
intriguing explanations
for left-handedness was
offered by the late
Dr. Norman Geschwind of Boston.
His theories suggest that
handedness is determined long
before birth, and the determining
factor is testosterone,
the male hormone.

It is known that during gestation,
if enough testosterone reaches
the fetus, it will temporarily
inhibit the development of
the right-handed brain,
giving the left-handed brain
a head start.

Result: a left-handed baby.

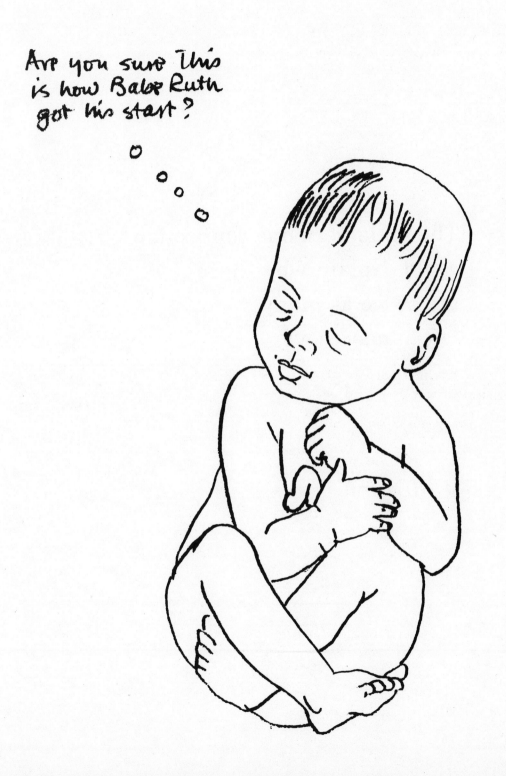

The male hormone connection
could explain why there
are twice as many
left-handed boys
as girls.

Dr. Geschwind's studies
also suggest that
left-handers are more
likely to have allergies
than right-handers.

But they appear to be less susceptible to infection and possibly to certain kinds of cancer.

No doubt about it—
left-handers are different
from right-handers—
they think differently,
they have different skills,
they even behave differently—
but they are in every way
equal . . . and sometimes
maybe superior . . . to the
right-handed majority.

What's even more certain
is that for the first time

in history, we are just now
entering the

It's an era when left-handed thinking is at a premium.

Four of the five designers
of the original Macintosh
computer were left-handed.

It's a time when the law
has ruled that left-handers
have rights, too!

In Woodbridge, Illinois, a jury
awarded $136,700 to a
left-handed clerk who was
ordered to check out groceries
with her right hand.

It's a time when
educators have come
to understand the
unique importance
of left-handers.

Juniata College in Darby, Pennsylvania, offers a special scholarship exclusively reserved for left-handers.

As the human race stands
poised on the threshold of the
next great frontier, where the
need for spatial, creative
thinking and planning will

be of crucial importance,
there is already evidence that
left-handers will be at the
forefront of the adventure. After
centuries of prejudice and indifference . . .

Left-handers are having
the last laugh.